DATING

PATRICIA RYON QUIRI

♥ ♥ ♥ ♥ **Dating** ♥ ♥ ♥ ♥

DRAWINGS BY ANNE CANEVARI GREEN

FRANKLIN WATTS
NEW YORK LONDON TORONTO SYDNEY 1989
A VENTURE BOOK

Library of Congress Cataloging-in-Publication Data

Quiri, Patricia Ryon.
Dating / by Patricia Ryon Quiri.
p.   cm.—(A Venture book)
Bibliography: p.
Includes index.
Summary: Discusses various aspects of dating for the
adolescent
including group dating, crushes, love, rejection, and going
steady.
ISBN 0-531-10806-6
1. Dating (Social customs)—Juvenile
literature.   2. Adolescence—
Juvenile literature.   [1. Dating (Social
customs)   2. Conduct of
life.]   I. Title.
HQ801.Q57   1989
646.7'7—dc20   89-5709   CIP   AC

CONTENTS

For my sons Rob, Brad, and C.J.

Seek love from within yourselves,
For once you find it,
It is for others to share.

I love you,
Mom

INTRODUCTION

Girls, boys, school, telephone calls, parties, dates. Exciting times are awaiting you. Confusing times are awaiting you. One minute you are happy, the next minute you are unhappy. All sorts of changes are going on inside of you, the preteen-physical changes as well as emotional ones. These changes occur earlier in some people, at a later age for others. Whenever these changes begin within *you*, that is the right time. The time of life we are discussing is called adolescence. It is the period of time between childhood and young adulthood. It is a confusing time because in many ways you are still a child, but in other ways you already have some adultlike ideas and responsibilities. You want to experience some independence. You want to take charge of yourself and be a part of the decision-making process in your life. This is an important part of growing up. Decision making fosters independence, which helps prepare you for adulthood.

Parents often have a difficult time giving their children independence. It is hard for parents to let go. After all, to them you are still (and probably always will be) "their little girl or boy." Adolescence is a signal to your parents that you are beginning to grow up. They also realize that they are not getting any younger!

Undoubtedly there will be some rough times between you and your parents during this period and even between your sisters or brothers and you. At one moment you and your brother or sister may be fighting like cats and dogs; the next moment you might be asking your mom or dad's permission to take the bus to the mall with a group of your friends. Your parents may question whether you are mature enough to do this. This time of childlike behavior mixed with adultlike wants is very normal for you, the young teen.

Adolescence is also the time of your life when you seriously start to notice the opposite sex. That boy next door may not seem like the nerd he seemed to be only last year. Or the girl who sits next to you in homeroom actually seems to have gotten kind of cute over the past few months. Sometimes you get a funny feeling inside you when you start liking someone of the opposite sex. You might not know what to say to that person or how to act around him or her. You might find yourself saying rather stupid things and you may even act kind of silly. This is all perfectly normal. After all, these feelings are new to you. Everyone goes through this during adolescence. As time goes on, you will become more sure of yourself and more confident in your relationships with the opposite sex.

Adolescence, independence, and a new-found interest in members of the opposite sex will eventually lead you to a fun-filled, exciting, and sometimes anxious period in your life—dating time. Dating gives you the opportunity to explore new friendships. Rather than limiting your circle of friends to members of your own sex, you will widen that circle with new friends and new interests. Some girls and boys are ready to do this sooner than others.

When is dating right for you? Since everyone is different and everyone goes through adolescence at varying speeds, it really depends on you, your friends, and, of course, parental permission. In the following pages, we talk about girls and boys and some of the changes that adolescence takes them through. We'll explore the world of dating— from being yourself and how to ask someone out to group dating and single dating. Tips on how to meet your date's parents are discussed, as well as what "going steady" means. Ideas on how to make "dating" or group fun money are offered, as well as lots of other interesting information on the subject of dating.

So . . . find some privacy, curl up in your favorite chair, and enjoy reading about dating.

CHAPTER

ADOLESCENCE
BRINGS CHANGES

One of the first signs of adolescence in girls is the growth spurt. Somewhere between the ages of nine and fourteen you may suddenly notice how tall you've become. Your breasts will begin to develop and you may need to wear a bra for support. Some girls develop earlier than others. If you are one of the "early bloomers," keep in mind that everyone else will eventually catch up to you. Perhaps you develop later than your friends, but you want to wear a bra because the other girls do. Special "training" bras are available. Don't be embarrassed to discuss this with your mother. It might be important to you to wear what other girls are wearing, especially when changing for gym in the locker room.

Another physical change that takes place during adolescence is the growth of pubic hair and underarm hair. You may even notice more hair on your legs and arms. You might want to remove the hair on your legs and the hair under your arms by shaving. Ask your mother for advice before removing it.

A significant body change in girls during adolescence is the onset of the menstrual period. The reason females have periods (monthly bleeding that passes out of the body through the vagina) is because every month a special lining forms inside the uterus. The uterus is a female organ where a baby can grow and be nourished. Each month a lining inside the uterus forms in order to prepare this organ for the nourishment of a baby. However, a baby can not form unless a girl or a woman is sexually active. So, if a female is not pregnant, the lining inside her uterus is shed, and then she has her period.

The blood from the uterine lining trickles out of the uterus, and flows down through the vagina and out of a female's body. The amount of blood that comes out is actually rather small, although it might seem to be a lot to you. The amount of blood can range from one or two tablespoons to about one cup. However, that amount of bleeding will not take place all at one time. Your period will last anywhere from two to seven days. When you first begin to menstruate your periods will most likely be irregular. They might occur every three, four, or five weeks, or you may even skip a few months between periods. When you become "regular," your period will come around every twenty-eight days. What is regular for you might be entirely different from what is regular for your best friend. Just remember, everyone is different. It's a good idea to keep track of your period on a calendar, so when it becomes fairly regular (which could take a couple of years), you will know when to expect it.

Sometimes girls refer to their periods as "the curse" or "my friend" or "that time of month."

Having your period may sound like an inconvenience to you or perhaps even like something you never want to experience. But every girl will begin menstruating sooner or later. It is a sign of approaching womanhood, and when it happens to you it will probably make you feel rather special. Your body has reached sexual maturity and you now have the capacity to bear children. In other words, once you have your period, you are capable of getting pregnant if you are sexually active.

Many different sanitary protection items for females are available in stores. It's a good idea to be prepared for your period before it begins. Speak to your mother (if she hasn't already brought up the subject) about getting several different types of sanitary napkins (also called pads) and/or tampons to have on hand. You might want to carry a small sanitary napkin in your purse in case you get your period while you are away from home. Otherwise, several layers of toilet paper folded over can be used as a makeshift pad in case of an emergency. You should experiment with the various types of sanitary protection to see which type best suits your needs. Remember your good personal hygiene routine (refer to Chapter 2) when you are menstruating. Daily bathing is especially important at this time and will make you feel more refreshed.

Every girl will undergo these physical changes that have been discussed. You may wonder when they will happen to you. This is something no one can predict. Every girl matures differently. These changes can begin as early as when you are nine, or they might not begin until you are sixteen. Finding out when your mother started developing might give you some indication as to when you might begin, as heredity is a factor. Many girls these days, however, seem to be maturing at an earlier age than their mothers did.

Physical changes that take place in adolescent boys usually occur anywhere between the ages of eleven and sixteen. Some boys may start to develop at an early age, whereas others may develop later. Adolescent boys also go through a growth spurt. You may notice the pants you bought last month look more like jams on you. Even before this rather sudden growth spurt, you may have noticed that your genitals were getting bigger. Boys, like girls, will begin to grow hair in the pubic region, under the arms, and on the face. You might notice more hair on your arms and legs. Some of you will grow hair on your chest and perhaps some will grow hair on your back. Your body muscles will begin to develop and your shoulders will get broader.

During adolescence your voice will begin to change; it will become lower. During this process, your voice may "crack" every so often as you speak. This may be embarrassing to you, but every boy goes through this phase.

A significant body change in boys during adolescence is having an erection followed by an ejaculation. When a boy's penis becomes hard and stiff, it is referred to as having an erection. The penis gets bigger—longer as well as wider. This happens because the tissue in the penis fills with more blood than it normally contains. An erection might occur when you think about sexual things or it may occur when you touch your penis. Sometimes it happens for no reason at all.

When a boy or a man has an erection, his penis sticks out from his body. You've probably experienced having an erection, but perhaps didn't know what it was called or why it was happening. Baby boys, little boys, adolescence boys, young men, and grown men have them. It is part of being a male. However, sometime during adolescence you will experience an ejaculation after an erection. An ejaculation is a "spitting out" or "spewing forth" of fluid from the tip of the penis. This fluid is not urine. It is made up of semen and sperm and is a sticky, milky-colored substance. It comes out in spurts. You might think that sounds sort of weird, and you might wonder why this happens. Once you have had an ejaculation it means your body has reached sexual maturity and you have the capacity to father children. In other words, you are capable of getting a girl pregnant if you are sexually active.

Your body is now producing sperm, which, if united with an egg from the body of a female, will create a new life—the beginning of a baby. The only way you can create a baby is by having sexual intercourse and ejaculating into a girl's vagina, or by ejaculating near a girl's vagina when clothes do not provide a barrier. (In other words, when you are both nude below the waist.) Sperm are fast movers, and if deposited by the vaginal opening, they can easily swim into the vagina.

Sometimes boys experience their first ejacuation during the night when they are asleep. This is called a "wet dream." It might feel as though you urinated in your bed. You might be upset or embarrassed by it. Having a wet dream is nothing to be ashamed of. It is a perfectly natural and normal occurrence that most boys go through. You may not remember what you were dreaming about, but it might have been a sexual dream. Wet dreams occur so your body can produce and store new sperm. It's your body's way of getting rid of the old sperm to make room for the new sperm. Having an ejaculation is a sign of approaching manhood for boys, just as having a period is a sign of nearing womanhood for girls.

All of these physical changes will occur in boys, although everyone develops at his own rate. You may want to ask your father when he started going through these changes. Keep in mind, however, that that does not necessarily mean you will develop at the same age or speed as your father did. Heredity is a factor, but each individual is different. Boys, too, seem to be developing at an earlier age these days than perhaps their fathers or grandfathers.

We have discussed the physical changes that take place in boys and girls during adolescence only to a limited extent. For an in-depth discussion on this subject, you might want to read the book *Puberty: The Story of Growth and Change,* that goes with this series on teen development. However, it was necessary to have touched upon some of these changes as they go hand-in-hand with the emotional changes that preteens go through.

CHAPTER

♥ two ♥

PERSONAL
HYGIENE

As your body develops from that of a child to one of an adult, so do your feelings about the opposite sex. You are ready to make new friendships with a whole different group of people. Let's talk about how you can get a boy or a girl to notice you.

First and foremost, you must practice good personal hygiene. Personal hygiene is taking care of yourself so you are clean and you look your best. This does not mean you have to wear the latest fads in fashion or look as if you belong on the cover of a teen magazine. What it does mean is daily bathing or showering. Washing with soap and water is very important at this age. As your body undergoes its physical changes, you may notice you sweat or perspire more. Your sweat glands tend to be quite active at this time. Very often when you perspire there is an odor to it. If this seems to be a problem for you, and if daily bathing doesn't help the odor, you might want to use some corn-starch or powder. Deodorants and antiperspirants are also available for underarm use. Girls

might want to shave the hair under the arms if there is an abundance of it. Sometimes the hair traps in odors as you perspire.

Both girls and boys may have to wash their hair more frequently than before because of those active sweat glands. They tend to make your hair "oily" or greasy-looking. These same glands can also be the cause of pimples cropping up every so often, an unfortunate part of adolescence. Some kids have more of a problem with this than others, and boys seem to get harder hit, but just about everyone gets pimples now and then. Pimples are another reason to wash well with soap and water. If you have a big problem with your skin, you might consider seeing a dermatologist, a skin doctor.

Keeping yourself clean not only makes you look good on the outside, but it will also make you feel good on the inside. It might mean that you will have to get up a little earlier in the morning or miss a TV show at night, but your efforts will be well worth it. That girl you've been wanting to ask to a movie is more likely to notice you (and more likely to say yes) if you are neat and clean. And that cute boy you sit next to just might pay more attention to you if you are fresh-smelling and tidy. Your efforts toward good personal hygiene certainly can't hurt you; they can only help.

Another grooming habit worth mentioning is taking care of your mouth and teeth, practicing good oral hygiene. Have you ever sat next to someone, who, after he started talking, you wished he hadn't? Bad breath is a real turn-off. Who wants to sit and talk to someone whose breath smells bad? Proper brushing and flossing of your teeth should help that problem. Your dental checkups will also benefit from this. Clean teeth also make for a prettier or more handsome smile.

Have you ever heard the expression "You are what you eat"? Everything you eat has an effect on you. If you are constantly eating junk food, sweets, and ice cream, it will probably show up in bad skin tone or excess weight. Because your body is growing and changing at a fast rate, it is important to eat properly and drink lots of water. This will help your complexion as well as your overall health. So instead of reaching for that candy bar, grab a piece of fruit.

Keeping your nails well manicured and clean should also be part of your daily routine. Girls might want to use nail polish. If you are a nail biter, now is the time to stop. After all, who wants to hold hands with a person who chews his or her nails down to the quick?

Some girls at this age like to experiment with a bit of makeup. It's best to get permission from your parents first, so they don't go into shock when they see the results of your experiments. Makeup can be fun to use, but remember to go easy on it. A soft natural look will turn more boys' heads than a lot of gloppy, heavy makeup.

Generally, boys don't need to shave until later in adolescence. However, if you are a boy who develops facial hair early and you are bothered by the so-called peach fuzz, ask your dad for his opinion (and perhaps a lesson or two) on shaving. This is strictly a personal decision, one to be made by you and your mother or father.

Now that you are on the road to good personal hygiene—looking good and feeling good—what else can you do to make boys or girls notice you? What are some ways to make friends with members of the opposite sex?

CHAPTER

MAKING
NEW FRIENDS

Your feelings about friends will probably change during this period of your life. You may have had a best friend throughout elementary school. After entering junior high school, you might not see much of each other anymore. Both of you have made new friends, and your outside interests have started taking shape. That's normal and natural. You will always have the memories of your childhood friend who was very important to you at that point in your life.

It is equally important to have friends at this next stage. When you were younger, you were very dependent on your mother and father. You wanted to spend a lot of time with them and do things that pleased them. As you journey through adolescence, you will become less dependent on your parents and more dependent on your friends. You want to spend more time with your peer group. It is very important for you to be accepted by them. This is very normal. Everyone wants to be liked and everyone wants to be popular. There may be times when you wish you were a little kid again and not have the worries or the pressures of an adolescent. Again, these are very normal feelings and everyone feels them at times during his or her teen years.

Popularity is easy for some people to attain. Those people are naturally outgoing and friendly. It is easy for them to make conversation and to have a ready smile. However, friends are needed by people of all social strata and by people of all ages. Good friendships are important to one's mental health. They make a person feel whole and complete. Usually one can count his or her close friends on one hand. It is difficult to have many close friends, because there just isn't enough time in everyday life to be extremely close with many people. You might belong to a particular clique at school that is composed of several people. However, within that social group you may have one or two "best friends."

Best friends feel equal to one another and can share secrets. Best friends feel comfortable around each other and often share the same values and ideas. Best friends are usually those who are with each other frequently—whether they live in the same neighborhood, share many classes together, are on the same teams, belong to the same clubs, etc. Best friends accept each other for what they are. While he or she may not always share the same ideas, close friends accept and value each other's opinions.

Close friendships require a certain responsibility to one another—caring, sharing, trusting, advising, and being there for one another. This is a responsibility that is easy to carry out when you care very much for a friend.

Good friendships withstand arguments. They

withstand the passage of time. Even though you and your best friend may be separated for a while, once you are back together, it doesn't feel like any time has passed.

Best friends are not jealous of one another, but instead they bring out the best in each other. Usually best friends are those of the same sex; however, this is not a rule without exception. A girl and a boy can be very close friends without having a romantic relationship.

Every friendship goes through problems, but a close friendship is one that can iron out differences and usually become stronger from those differences.

Let's now discuss ways of making friends with people of the opposite sex.

One way to meet people and make more friends of the opposite sex is by getting involved in activities in and out of school. Make yourself known. It's more fun and perhaps easier to do this with a friend. If you enjoy sports, why not join a team? Perhaps you'd like to attend school sports programs or become involved in your church or synagogue youth program. Many schools have dances for kids your age. Sometimes communities sponsor social events for young people. When you enter junior high school, there usually are a number of clubs and activities you can join—drama, debate, band, chorus. Figure out what your strengths and interests are and join a group that will help you cultivate them. This will help develop your self-confidence, which, in turn, will help develop new friendships.

There are lots of ways to become involved and meet new friends if you want to. It just takes that first step. Sure, it might be a little scary. You might wonder if you'll fit into the group, but you'll never know unless you try. So, give it a chance. It's fun to meet new people and it's fun to be busy.

Very often when a girl likes a boy, or when a boy likes a girl, he or she doesn't know how to act or what to say. This is understandable, because after all, these are new and different feelings you are experiencing. When you were small, around four or five, you probably had friends of the opposite sex. You enjoyed doing and playing the same sort of things. You really didn't think of your friend as being a boy or a girl. You just had fun together. Then, as you got a little older, perhaps around six or seven, you might have gone through the "hate" stage. "Yuck, I hate girls!" or "Ooh, do I have to invite him? He's a boy!" However, at the age of ten, eleven, or twelve, a boy might not think girls are so bad and vice versa. It's funny how feelings change. It's all part of the growing-up process.

If a boy likes a girl, he might show it in a rather odd way. He might tease her, or pull her hair, or "accidentally" bump into her. He is unsure of how to pay attention to someone he likes. The same can be true of girls. As your friendships with the opposite sex increase, so will your knowledge of how to handle yourself. The main thing is to be yourself. This is not always easy. When you are in a new situation, let's say at a party for both boys and girls, you might be nervous and wonder how to act. You might get giggly with a friend. A normally outgoing boy or girl suddenly may become shy.

You are constantly learning about yourself from new situations. This all helps to shape you and your personality. If you think you are too shy, too loud, too sensitive, or perhaps too short-tempered, you can try to make some changes within yourself. You will be making decisions—some will be right and others will be wrong. The important thing is you learn about yourself from your mistakes and your successes. You are a special person, and there is no one in the world just like you. There is no one who looks just like you (unless, of course, you are an identical twin) and there is no one who acts or feels exactly the same way you do.

This brings up an important subject—self-image. Self-image is how you feel about yourself. If you feel good about yourself and you like and respect yourself, you will have the ability to like and respect others. This might sound sort of funny to you. It might sound like a "stuck-up" attitude. But having a positive self-image simply means knowing you are a good friend to have and a person worth knowing. How do you develop a positive self-image? It has actually been forming since you were a baby. Most people develop a positive self-image from their families, who have brought them up with love and respect.

By now you have a good sense of what is right and what is wrong. Treating others the way you want to be treated is a good rule to follow. Being friendly, saying "hi," and having a smile are all ways to open the door to new friendships.

CHAPTER

GROUP DATING

As you enter the preteen years, you may become interested in dating, or even interested in daydreaming about dating. It's fun to talk with your best friend about boys and girls whom you think are nice. Some boys and girls get interested in doing so sooner than others. Typically, girls are apt to be ready sooner than boys to embark upon this new adventure. Keep in mind that you are perfectly normal if you have little or no interest in members of the opposite sex right now. However, since you are reading this book, one can safely assume you are somewhat interested in the subject of dating.

Some girls and boys begin to date at a young age, whereas others don't date until they are eighteen or so. When is it right for you? That depends on a number of factors. Probably the most influential factor is your parents. Even though you may think you are ready to date, your parents may not agree. Some parents put an age requirement on dating—perhaps when you are fourteen, fifteen, or sixteen. That might seem like forever to you to have to wait, but there are alternatives. Most pre-teens do not actually go on "single" dates anyway. You are still learning about yourself. Most kids at this age just wouldn't feel comfortable on a single date. There are other ways to get together with a group of girls and boys.

One way of doing this is to plan a party. You must first get permission from your parents and settle on a date, time, and how many kids you can invite. Sometimes it's easier and more fun to throw a party with a friend. Two or three heads plan-ning together can come up with more ideas than just one person. At this age, it's a good idea to have specific things to do at a party. This way the boys and girls will mingle with one another and won't feel too awkward. The last thing you want to happen is for the girls to be on one side of the room and the boys to be on the other side, and everyone feeling rather bored and silly.

One suggestion for a party might be a scaven-ger hunt. First divide the group into teams. (You as the party-giver get to choose who you want on your team. Maybe that nice boy in your science class or perhaps that girl next door.) Give each team a list of things it has to gather. If you know your neighbors, you could go door-to-door in search of these things. You might also include items you can find outside. The team that comes back first with the most things on its list it has gathered wins. This sort of activity is a good "ice breaker." When all teams have returned, there's bound to be plenty of conversation. Perhaps after that, have some snacks and play music.

Games such as Junior Pictionary® or Trivial Pursuit for Juniors® are also fun at parties and another good way to get the conversation and mingling started. Parties at which there are things to do help make boys and girls feel more at ease with one another. You'll also get great reviews from the kids. After having a party, it is always nice to hear, "Great party!" If your party is a success, other kids will be bound to feel confident enough to have parties at their houses.

Other ideas for get-togethers are biking, sledding, or beach parties (depending on the season). You could arrange for everyone to meet at a certain place with a bike, sled, or bathing suit, and before you know it the fun begins. A couple of adults might want to organize these parties. Arrange after sledding, for instance, to go back to someone's house for soft drinks or hot chocolate and snacks. For beach or lake parties, which are easy and fun, everyone provides the entertainment. There is so much to do—swim, sun, ride waves, walk, throw a Frisbee® or football. No one's house is involved and no one person is responsible for the get-together being a success or a flop.

Another way to get a group together could be a day at the park. Softball or volleyball games and picnicking are fun things to do with a large group.

Thus far, all the ideas discussed cost little, if any, money to do. (Unless you are the party-giver mentioned earlier.) Some parents might agree to spring for a party once in awhile. After all, having a busy preteen makes for a happy preteen. Besides, most parents want to get to know the kids with whom their children hang around.

A few other ideas for "group dating" (which simply means going places and doing things with a group of boys and girls) include: going to the movies, spending a day at the mall, bowling, roller skating, playing miniature golf, or going to a fair. These are all activities that require money and most likely transportation.

CHAPTER

EARNING MONEY
FOR DATING

So you would like to go to the roller rink with a group of your friends. Or you might want to take a special friend to the movies. Some of the things you'd like to do cost money. Are you going to "hit" Mom or Dad for some spending money? They may go for that occasionally, but more often than not, they'll probably say, "Why don't you earn your own money?" You may moan and groan a bit at hearing this, but actually you'll feel pretty good about watching the old piggy bank grow. Having your own money makes you feel pretty independent. So, how can you increase your cash flow?

Talk to your parents about getting an allowance. Discuss what you will do to earn it—make your bed, keep your room neat, take out the garbage, set the table, do the dishes, do the laundry, rake leaves, mow the grass, shovel the snow. There are lots of possibilities. Set an allowance that is fair to both you and your parents. Do your job well, and who knows? Maybe you'll get an increase in pay.

You are at the age at which you can be trained to baby-sit. Lots of parents would love to have a helper. You could probably earn between $1.00 and $2.00 an hour for starters. When you become more experienced, you might earn more. When you baby-sit, remember the children are your first responsibility. However, once the children are in bed, you should look around the house. Are there toys all over the place? Straighten up and put the toys away. Are there dishes by the sink or food strewn all over the floor from that toddler you are watching? Clean up a bit. All the extras you do after the kids are in bed will most likely earn you a tip from the parents. The harder you work at your job, the more money you will earn. You'll also be called back again. Names of good baby-sitters travel fast. You'll probably be recommended to other parents to sit for their children.

What about a paper route to earn some money? It's hard work and usually means working in the early hours, but it is a possible job opportunity. Again, if you do this, do it well. No one likes a soggy paper, and no one likes to hunt for the paper in the bushes or on the roof. Remember when you collect money for the paper, the girl or boy who provides good service often gets a tip.

Raking leaves, shoveling snow-packed driveways, mowing lawns—these are all ways to help your neighbors and increase your cash flow. Check first with your parents and then go to neighbors whom you know.

How about offering to collect a neighbor's mail when he or she is away? Or feed the cat? Or water the plants? There are many ways to make some money. Just remember, if you are going to take the responsibility of a job, do it well and provide the best service you can.

Now that you're all charged up to make your piggy bank grow, you might think, "So when will I have the time to go to the roller rink with my friends?" Or you might think, "Forget the friends, I'll just make some money!" Seriously, let's assume you have spending money and you are interested in doing things with your group of friends. You have some ideas of what to do, where to go, how to get a group of kids together, and a rough idea of how much these things cost. How can you get permission from your parents to do them?

CHAPTER

♥ **SIX** ♥

PARENTAL
PERMISSION
TO DATE

When seeking permission from your parents to be a part of group activities, keep in mind these three words: communication, honesty, and trust. Talk to your parents. It may be hard for them to realize you are growing up and your interests are broadening, as is your social situation. Introduce your friends to your parents. Have them get to know each other. If you have been invited to a party, let your mom or dad know where it will be and who is going to be there. It's important to parents to know your friends and be comfortable with them. It's just as important for parents to know there is another adult supervising activities such as these.

Always be honest with your mother and father. Honesty promotes trust and good strong relationships. If you are honest about where you are going and with whom you are going, you will most likely be given more independence. Being dishonest, or lying, can only get you into trouble. Surely everyone knows what "being grounded" means. (For those of you who don't, it means you can't do

anything or go anywhere for a certain period of time.)

If you get permission to go out with a group of friends, you will probably be given a curfew. A curfew is a specific time at which you are to be home. This could be a daytime curfew. Perhaps you have plans to take the bus to the mall with a group of friends. Your mother tells you she wants you home by 4:30. Be responsible. Check the bus schedule to allow the right amount of time to get you home by your curfew. If you find you are going to be late, have sense enough to call your house and let your mom or dad know. Parents have a tendency to worry, not because they like to nag, but because they love their children. Being home by your curfew or calling if you will be late demonstrates that you are responsible enough to handle yourself in a mature manner. The rewards of sticking to a curfew will probably be permission to do this sort of thing again.

Curfews are also (and especially) given at night. Your curfew will probably depend on a number of things: where you are going, what you are doing, with whom you are going, and means of transportation. At this age, means of transportation would most likely be parents or older siblings, unless you are within walking distance of your destination. Make sure the curfew is agreed upon among all parents in the group. If you are taking public transportation, do so with some friends, because traveling in a group is safer than traveling alone.

CHAPTER

♥ seven ♥

DATING AND
PEER PRESSURE

Another important subject to discuss when you are "group dating" or doing things with a group of girls and boys is peer pressure, going along with the crowd. It is important for girls and boys to feel accepted by their peers. But to what extent do you go to gain this acceptance? Let's talk about a few "for instances."

Let's suppose you are part of a group at school which is really popular—the "in" crowd. The members of the group are quite active in sports programs. Some of the girls have boyfriends and some of the boys have girlfriends. How do these group members treat other kids who are not part of their clique? Do they tend to ignore them or make fun of them?

Every school has certain cliques. This is very typical and all part of the social process. But do remember everyone has feelings and feelings can be hurt. Just because someone in the group makes fun of another person outside the clique doesn't mean it's right. Putting someone down says something about you. It says you are insecure. You certainly don't make friends by hurting other people. Try to put yourself in another person's shoes. How would you feel if you were the one being made fun of? Showing compassion toward others, even when it means not conforming to the views of group, shows you are a caring person. Sometimes this is hard to do. However, you will probably find others in your group who feel the same way you do. Once the initial step is taken, others are sure to follow.

Another instance of peer pressure within a group is involvement with cigarettes, drugs, and alcohol. This sort of peer pressure can be very dangerous to your health and life if you decide to go along with the crowd. Here's a pretend situation. A bunch of you get together at an uncrowded park for a picnic and a game of softball. One of the most popular guys pulls out a joint (marijuana cigarette) and offers it to everyone to share. A few kids look nervous; some go along with him and smoke it. It's passed to you. What are you going to do? You know that drugs are illegal and dangerous. You know you'd get "what for" and probably be grounded by your parents if they ever found out you tried drugs. However, you don't want the rest of the group to think you don't belong. But consider this—do they like you for what you are, or do they include you because you'll go along with whatever they do?

Friends who won't like you because you don't try something or because you have different opinions about things aren't really friends at all. It is somewhat easier today to "just say no" because of all the attention the media has given drugs and alcohol. Kids are educated at an early age about the dangers of using drugs and alcohol. So think: is it worth risking your health or perhaps your life for the approval of a few people? As is usually the case, there will be more people who, like you, do not want to go along with the crowd. So once again, do not be afraid to defend what you feel is right. True friends will not bully you into trying something like drugs or alcohol, but will respect your views.

Let's take a look at another example of peer pressure. In the following situation, three girls go to the beach and meet three boys with whom they spend the day.

Susan met Cindy and Beth at the bus stop. They were all going to spend the day at the beach, picnicking, sunbathing, swimming, and hopefully meeting some cute boys.

After a thirty-minute bus ride, the girls found themselves lugging their gear toward the swelling surf.

"Look at those waves!" exclaimed Cindy. "I can't wait to ride one in!"

"Me too," agreed Cindy's best friend, Beth. "Let's hurry and find a good spot for this stuff."

"Preferably near some cute-looking boys," grinned Susan.

"You're so boy-crazy, Susan!" laughed Cindy. "Is that all you can think about?"

"Can you think of anything better?" joked Susan.

The girls settled on a spot of beach near the water. After spreading their towels and parking their coolers under a rented umbrella, they raced for the foamy ocean.

Twenty minutes of swimming and body surfing passed. Susan turned to her friends to say she was going to sunbathe.

"We'll be there in a little while, Susan," Cindy told her.

Susan returned to where they had spread their

towels, noticing that the water was creeping up on their spot.

"Oh, nuts," she muttered, stooping to pull her beach bag to drier ground.

"Can I give you a hand?" inquired the most gorgeous suntanned boy Susan had ever seen.

"Sure," she replied, trying hard not to stare. "My friends are still in the water swimming."

"Oh, yeah?" responded the boy, whose name was Jimmy. "How many friends do you have with you?"

"Two," answered Susan. "Here they come now. Hey, Cindy and Beth! I'd like you to meet Jimmy. He saved our towels from being wrapped around Jaws!"

"Why don't we just move your stuff to where my buddies and I are sitting?" suggested Jimmy.

They moved the girls' things, and, safe from the water's edge, the girls discovered Jimmy had two friends with him. Introductions made, they started to make conversation.

The afternoon passed quickly. After the beach began to empty, Jimmy turned to the girls and said, "Would any of you like some coke?"

"Oh, no thanks," replied Susan. "I think we still have some in our cooler."

"Not *that* kind of coke, silly . . . cocaine."

"Oh," said Susan, a look of surprise and disappointment crossing her face.

"Not for me," spoke up Cindy. "That stuff is dangerous, not to mention illegal."

"Yeah," replied Beth, echoing Cindy's feelings.

"How 'bout you, good-lookin'?" coaxed Jimmy, as he flashed a handsome smile at Susan.

Susan cast an uneasy glance at her friends. They had already refused Jimmy's offer, but would Jimmy still like her if she said no as well?

Susan caught the looks her friends were giving her. She really liked this guy and she hoped to see him again. If she said no to his offer of cocaine, he might think she was too straight for him. However, she did not want to get mixed up with drugs. She quickly thought up a dumb lie and said, "Oh, no thanks. The last time I did coke my nose bled for two hours."

Whether you just say no, as Cindy and Beth did, or you make up a lie like Susan, make sure you don't get involved with drugs or alcohol. Susan did what she considered smart. She didn't want Jimmy to think she was too straight for him, so she made up a lie. That was okay. That was her way of taking charge and saying no.

Responding to pressure from your peers is never easy, but it is certainly easier to deal with when you have one or two close friends who share the same values as you do. You may even find you want to break away from a particular clique and seek other friends who are more compatible with your standards and your way of thinking.

One more big topic on the subject of peer pressure to discuss is the issue of sex. As your body and mind mature from that of a child to a young adult, you will become aware of physical attractions toward the opposite sex. If you are a girl, you may be attracted to a boy who is particularly handsome. If you are a boy, you might be attracted to a girl who is really pretty. You may wonder what it would be like to hold hands with or even kiss that person. It is normal if you have already experienced these feelings and it is just as normal if you haven't yet felt them. However, don't let peer pressure push you into doing something physical you do not want to do.

What about kissing or "making out"? If a boy or girl wants to make out with you and you don't want to, again, just say no. You are the one who must live with yourself and your reputation. If doing what the crowd is doing is not comfortable for you, stick up for what you feel is right. Your body belongs to you and only you. *No one* has the right to force you into doing something you don't want to do. Remember about good and bad touches. A good touch is one that makes you feel good or comfortable. A bad touch is one that makes you feel bad or uncomfortable. If a boyfriend or a girlfriend wants you to make out and it makes you feel uncomfortable, say no.

What about petting? Petting is another term that has to do with sex. Generally, it means touching. You might pet your dog or cat. That means touching your animal in a way that it likes. When girls and boys "pet," it usually involves touching in "private" places. If a boy and girl are sexually attracted to each other, they may experiment with their aroused sexual feelings. A boy might touch a girl's breasts. Each of them might touch the other below the waist. Sometimes the issue of sex is talked about in terms of "bases." Boys or girls might ask one another, "What base did you get to?" First base means kissing, second base means petting above the waist, third base means petting below the waist, and a home run means having sexual intercourse.

Sexual intercourse is the act of having sex, which is also called "making love." A male's penis becomes hard (erect) and he inserts it into a female's vagina. Moving it around creates a nice feeling for the man and woman. Usually all this moving around will result in an ejaculation by the man. Women do not experience ejaculation; however, the vagina does get moist during sexual arousal, and the woman may experience an orgasm.

Sexual intercourse is the means by which nature intended the human species to continue. Pregnancies can occur from having sex. It's up to you to make your own sexual decisions. Having sexual intercourse with someone is not only a physical experience, but a highly emotional one. When a man and a woman are in love, they like to express the depth of their emotional love with their bodies. Making love is the closest physical way possible to be intimate with someone. Many people believe this experience should be shared only by people who are mature enough to handle it and who truly love one another. After all, it is a very intimate and private way of expressing love.

Sex is not a game. Your boyfriend or girlfriend might try to coax you into having sex by saying, "If you really love me, you'll do this." Does that sound like someone who honestly cares about you and your feelings? Know where to draw the line. Make the decision that you are comfortable with and that will leave you with your self-respect.

A lot of times boys like to brag about what sexual things they have done with girls. Sometimes they even make them up. Word gets around pretty quickly about girls and boys. Sometimes the girl who readily has sex gets called for many dates. However, when it comes time for a more meaningful and lasting relationship, it will probably be the girl who has a good self-image and who is fun to be with (and not just anxious to jump into bed) who gets called. Again, remember you are the one who has to live with the reputation you make for yourself, whether you are a boy or a girl. Remember your self-respect. If you don't feel comfortable doing what a boy or girl wants you to do, say no. If you are called a prude, why should you care? When someone says, "everyone else is doing it," tell him or her you are not like everyone else. If he or she doesn't want to see you after that, you can safely assume that he or she was only interested in one thing—seeing how far you would go. That's not what a friendship is all about.

The next example is about a boy named Mike and a girl named Sandy. They have been dating for a month and get along very well. You will find that each of them has very similar reactions to the issue of sex.

"Great movie, huh?" remarked Mike, munching on a greasy french fry.

"Yeah, it was good," agreed Sandy as she took the last bite of her cheeseburger. "What do you want to do now? It's only 9:30 and I don't have to be home until 11:00."

"Well, we could take a drive down to the lake," suggested Mike.

"Okay, just as long as I'm in by 11:00 or my dad will have a bird."

The two walked hand in hand back to Mike's car.

"This has been a fun night, Mike," said Sandy, and impulsively she kissed him. Grinning down at her, Mike replied, "It's not over yet."

They drove silently to the lake, each engrossed in his or her own thoughts.

After parking the car, Mike asked, "Do you want to walk around or would you rather sit in the car and talk?"

"Oh, let's take a short walk," Sandy replied as she pushed open the car door. The lakefront was deserted except for a few couples who were interested only in themselves. Sandy's teeth chattered when the wind picked up as they neared the water.

"Cold?" asked Mike. "Here, take my jacket." He

wrapped the coat around Sandy and then took her in his arms. His lips met hers and they kissed. "Let's go back to the car," Mike murmured. "It's warmer in there."

Sandy and Mike strolled back slowly. Sandy really liked Mike a lot, but she was wondering if coming to the lake was such a good idea. She hoped he didn't expect too much of her sexually. Mike, on the other hand, was thinking similar thoughts. "She's the one who first kissed me," he mused to himself. "And she didn't pull away when I just kissed her. I wonder what she wants me to do."

They slid into the front seat, both with unanswered questions on their minds.

"Why don't we just go back to my house and have some hot chocolate?" suggested Sandy suddenly.

"Sounds good to me," agreed Mike quickly. He felt a tremendous amount of pressure lift off his shoulders.

Except for a stolen kiss here or there and perhaps light petting, most kids are afraid to become sexually active. As you saw in the previous situation, the boy and girl were both hesitant to go any further than handholding and kissing. Sometimes boys as well as girls think sex is expected of them. While dating can lead to sexual experiences, it doesn't have to. If a boy and girl have a mutual respect for one another and know each other's boundaries, a good time can be had without involving sex. Having sex is a way of trying to achieve closeness for some girls and boys who do not get love and affection from their families. Many times, however, it involves a "one-night stand" and not real love. Then, unfortunately, one's self-respect goes downhill, and the people involved may feel really weird and uncomfortable when they see each other again. Love and sex are not the same thing.

Sexual contact—kissing, petting, sexual intercourse—is not a game. It is not a race among your friends to see who has done what first. The issue of sex is not only physical, but also very emotional. Teens are developing and recognizing their sexuality at a younger age these days. Emotional maturity, however, is a much slower process. Hopefully, moral values have been instilled in you by your family, because ultimately you are the one to make your own sexual decisions. Learn the facts about sexually transmitted diseases. These are not to be taken lightly. Diseases you can contract by being sexually active include herpes, gonorrhea, syphilis, pubic lice, chlamydia, and, of course, the deadly disease AIDS. Some of these diseases can be treated and cured if detected early enough. However, there is no known cure yet for genital herpes. If one contracts AIDS, it is fatal. Teenage pregnancy can also be a consequence of being sexually active. A teenage girl who finds herself pregnant will face the wrenching, agonizing dilemma of what to do. And a teen boy who finds himself the potential father will also be in a difficult situation. So let your head rule your heart— be smart and make the right decisions.

CHAPTER

CRUSHES AND
TRUE LOVE

During adolescence you may develop a "crush" on someone. This crush may or may not be a mutual feeling between a girl and a boy. Crushes aren't really love. Sometimes you are attracted to members of the opposite sex who are popular. Crushes usually occur when you don't know the person very well, perhaps not at all. You might just like the way she or he looks. This is also a very normal part of growing up. It can be a lot of fun talking with your best friend about people to whom you are attracted. Crushes don't last a long time. You might have a crush on someone one week and think to yourself the next week, "What did I ever see in her?"

What about real love? As was mentioned earlier, love starts within yourself. Loving and respecting yourself makes you capable of loving and respecting others. The first people you loved were your parents. As you started to grow up, you might have had a special friend whom you loved. You had fun together, shared secrets, and enjoyed each other's company. If you work at it, you will continue to have these types of friendships throughout your life. These friendships do not necessarily have to be limited to members of one's own sex. Many people have strong relationships with people of the opposite sex that do not involve romantic love.

Romantic love or true love is not easy to understand. It's a special feeling between a boy and a girl or a man and a woman. It's a two-way street of give and take. It is sharing and trusting. It is having mutual respect for one another. It feels right when you are together. It also means working out problems together. True love usually lasts a long time. Adolescents are just beginning to experience feelings for members of the opposite sex. You might not encounter true love until high school, college, or perhaps not until later in your life. Dating different people as you mature will help you understand yourself and others better, and it will eventually lead you to know what qualities you find most appealing in a man or a woman.

CHAPTER

♥ **nine** ♥

SINGLE DATING

Suppose you really like this girl or boy and would like to spend some time alone with her or him. You want to get to know her or him better. How do you go about asking this person out? Once again, self-image and being yourself comes to mind. Most people like to be around someone who is sure of himself or herself and has a good self-image. So, gather your self-confidence and talk to your parents first. You will most likely need permission to go on a single date. Your parents will probably want to know all about the girl or boy you are interested in and will also want to know where you intend to take that person. You might get a bit impatient with your parents and their requests. You are growing up and becoming increasingly independent. If your parents agree to this date, you may need to ask for money and transportation. Try to understand that it really is within your parents' rights to ask these questions.

Let's assume you receive permission from your mother or father to ask someone out. The next

CALLING VANESSA FOR A DATE? HE WAS CALMER WHEN WE TOLD HIM HE HAD TO HAVE HIS APPENDIX OUT!

step is to ask that person. Should you call him or her? Should you ask him or her at school? This is a matter of personal choice. You may find that the telephone is easier. If you become nervous, the other person can't see you. If you turn a thousand shades of purple, the person won't know.

Asking someone out is a hard thing to do. There is always the nagging thought, "What if she says no?" or "I'll feel like a geek if he laughs at me." However, you'll never find out unless you try. So, once again, get the old self-confidence together and make that phone call. Remember your telephone manners. That may sound silly to you, but if his or her parent answers the phone, the person will be more impressed with, "Hello. This is Tom Smith. May I please speak to Julie?" (answer) "Thank-you"; rather than an abrupt, "Can I talk to Julie?" When someone of the opposite sex calls their son or daughter, parents are usually curious to know who it is.

Once you are over that hurdle, what will you do when the person to whom you wish to speak gets on the phone? Again remember your manners. Let's go back to our pretend situation with Tom Smith and Julie. Tom might say, "Hi, Julie. This is Tom Smith. Would you like to go to the movies with me on Friday night?" That is a nice way to ask someone out. How does this sound? "Hi, Julie. This is Tom Smith. You wouldn't want to go out with me Friday night, would you?" Try to sound positive. If you start off in a negative way, the person might think, "Gee, I really don't want to go out with him."

Let's look at some of the ways Julie might respond to Tom's invitation:

"Gee, Tom, that sounds great. I'll have to ask my mom first."

"I'd like to, Tom, but I already have plans. Maybe some other time."

"I'm sorry, Tom, but I don't want to."

The first response is going to make Tom feel like a million bucks. And from the way Julie responded, she probably feels like a million bucks that Tom called her. Response number two seems to be honest and direct. Julie made other plans but thinks it would work out another time. From what she said, Tom will probably feel confident enough to invite her out again. The third reply is bound to make Tom feel bad. Hopefully, it won't shatter his self-confidence. If someone says no to you, sure it's going to hurt. You might even feel kind of stupid. You may feel as though you never want to ask another person out again for fear of rejection. These are all normal reactions. But don't give up. As the old expressions go, "There are lots of fish in the sea" and "If at first you don't succeed, try try again." No one likes to be turned down, but don't dwell on it for too long. Maybe there is someone else you'd like to get to know better. If so, start the process again. Get back your confidence and go for it. Most boys and girls are flattered when someone asks them for a date, whether or not they say yes.

Let's return to our made-up situation about Tom and Julie. For the sake of taking you through a pretend date, let's say Julie gave Tom response number one. Tom is feeling on top of the world and so is Julie. She thinks Tom is a neat guy and is thrilled he asked her out. What Julie needs to do now is get permission from her parents. Assuming they feel Julie is old enough to date, they are going to want to know who Tom is, how old he is, where they are going, and how they will get there. Julie might feel as though she is getting the third degree, but her parents are concerned about her well-being and they are justified in these questions. Julie should be up-front and honest with them in order to maintain an open and trusting relationship. In doing so, she will most likely be given permission for future dates.

Back to our date. Julie got the okay from her parents. Since Tom is too young to drive, his dad is going to drop them off at the movie theater. First, they have to pick Julie up at her house. Tom is a little nervous; this is a normal way to feel. Tom has taken extra care in his grooming and personal hygiene routine. He wants to look his best. Julie is also nervous. She too has taken more time than usual in getting ready. It's time now for Tom to pick Julie up. How in the world is he going to act in front of her parents? From what you have read earlier in this book, what advice would you give Tom? Be polite, be confident, have good manners, and, above all, be himself. Practicing in front of a mirror is a good idea. Tom might say, "Hello, Mr. and Mrs. Baines. I'm Tom Smith. It's nice to meet you. Is Julie ready?" He's off to a good start, and the conversation takes off from there.

Usually young people are given a curfew or a time by which they must be home. As was mentioned in chapter six, if you are unable to make your curfew, call home. If the reason is valid, most parents will understand. When you go on a single date and use your parents as the means of transportation, you can be fairly sure you will be home on time. If you have an early curfew—say around 9:00—you might arrange to go out on your date during the late afternoon or early evening.

Other methods of transportation include taking taxi cabs (which are pretty expensive and perhaps not within young peoples' budgets), having an older sibling drive, or taking a bus or subway. Never hitchhike or take rides from people you do not know. That can be extremely dangerous.

So far the issue of dating might sound pretty intriguing to you. But what can you do if your parents absolutely flatly refuse to allow you to date until you are sixteen? You might ask them if you can invite a friend over to the house to watch a movie or play cards. This way your parents will be satisfied because you are home where they can supervise. You might not be totally thrilled because you'd rather be out, but it is a compromise. You get to be with that special person, even if it is a "home" date. Try it! You may be surprised at how much fun it turns out to be. Besides, you can't beat the cost.

Other places to go on a single date include: the movies, bowling, roller rink, pizza parlor, miniature golf, video arcade, parties, dances, sock-hops, shopping, beach, sporting events, concerts, out for a bite to eat, or a day at the park. There are endless possibilities. How about an evening when you and your date fix dinner for your parents? That might be a fun way for everyone to get to know each other.

CHAPTER

DATING AN
OLDER PERSON AND
BLIND DATES

Dating an older person is another issue that must be discussed with your parents. The teen's maturity level plays a big part in this discussion. Girls tend to be more mature than boys during the pre-teen and early teen years. They might think that boys their own age are rather immature. Girls might be asked out by boys who are one, two, or three grades ahead of them. Sometimes this also happens with boys.

If you do get permission to date an older person, you may get to meet more people—his or her friends. It might be fun to branch out with different friends. It could also mean that your "older" date might expect more from you. He or she might feel you should be able to stay out later. He or she may try to get past first base with you. Then again it could simply mean a good time and the beginning of a nice friendship. Ultimately, you are the one who has to assess the situation and decide if it is right for you.

Read what happens when Katie goes on a date with an older boy named Paul.

The home crowd roared with enthusiasm as the ball flew in the direction of the basket. Swish! The Jayhawks were up by two when the shrill buzzer signaled the end of the first half.

Seeking relief from the heat of the gym, Katie and Marie made their way to the lobby. A cool blast of air welcomed them as the lobby doors were pushed open.

"I'm dying of thirst. Let's go over to the water fountain," said Katie, rolling up the sleeves of her sweater. The girls zigzagged through the growing crowd.

"Umm. That tastes good," remarked Katie, gulping down the water. "My throat is parched."

"Excuse me, can I get a drink?" Katie straightened up and found herself looking into a handsome pair of sky-blue eyes.

"Sure, no problem," answered Katie.

After the boy quenched his thirst, he said to the girls, "What a game, huh? Do you go to this school?"

"Sure do," answered Marie. "We've got one of the best basketball teams in our league."

"Yeah, so do we," grinned the boy, whose name was Paul. The girls chatted with Paul during half-time and he asked them to join him in the bleachers. "A bunch of my buddies are sitting there. Why don't you come and meet them?"

"Why not?" answered Katie and Marie.

They squeezed into the bleachers next to Paul and his friends and they all enjoyed the second half of the game.

As they left the gymnasium, Paul turned to the

girls and asked, "Either of you going to the basketball conference?"

"When does it begin?" asked Marie.

"Next weekend," replied Paul. "Both of our schools are participating in it."

Katie was quick to say, "Yeah, I'm planning on going." She thought Paul was pretty nice and it would be fun to see him again. They exchanged phone numbers and said good-bye.

Three days passed and Katie didn't hear from Paul. She complained to Marie about it and her friend suggested she call him.

"He might think I'm too forward," stated Katie. "Besides, he probably wanted you to go with him."

"Oh, c'mon. He's a nice guy and all, but I sort of liked his friend Steve."

"Maybe we could double!" exclaimed Katie. "That would be radical!"

As it turned out, Katie finally got in touch with Paul, and they agreed to meet at the basketball conference, along with their friends Marie and Steve. The evening sped by. As they were leaving the school, Paul said, "You girls up for a party? A friend of ours is having a few people over. Why don't we check that out and then we'll take you home?"

Katie shrugged her shoulders as she looked at Marie. "Is that okay with you?"

"All right," responded Marie. "But I have to be home by 10:30."

"Ten-thirty!" exclaimed the boys. "Why so early?"

"I don't know. That's my curfew for tonight," answered Marie defensively.

"Mine too," added Katie in a small voice.

"You girls are juniors and you have to be in at 10:30?" asked Paul.

"Whoever said we were juniors?" asked Marie. "We're freshmen!"

"You're kidding!" said Steve in amazement. "Well, let's get going. We only have an hour and a half."

They jumped out of Paul's car after he pulled into his friend's driveway. The house was dimly lit. They heard soft music as they entered.

"Let's go downstairs and see what's happening," suggested Paul.

As they went down the stairs, Katie could make out three couples dancing slowly to the beat. She glanced around the darkened room and saw a few more couples scattered in various corners.

"What's everyone doing?" questioned Katie innocently.

"What do you think they're doing?" laughed Paul. "They're making out. Let's see if we can find a couch or something. Okay?"

Katie shuffled uneasily and thrust her hands into her pockets.

"You're so pretty, Katie. What's the matter? I thought you liked me."

"I do, Paul, but this is moving a little too fast for me," replied Katie. "Are there any adults around?"

"Nah, Pete's folks are away for the weekend," answered Paul.

"Oh, brother," groaned Katie. She was not allowed to go to any unchaperoned parties. She also felt uncomfortable in this situation. "Listen, Paul, I hate to be a party-pooper, but could you give Marie and me a lift home now? I don't think we really fit in here."

"Aw, c'mon," answered Paul. "Let's just stay for a few minutes. You and I can get to know each other better."

"Yeah, that's what I'm afraid of," Katie tried to joke. "But I'd rather get to know you somewhere where I can see you."

Paul seemed rather reluctant, but he and Steve took the girls home. Katie felt good about herself because she refused to stay in a situation that made her feel uneasy. Sometimes "older" dates may expect more from you, as you have seen in this example. If you find yourself in a similar situation and you feel uncomfortable, remember what Katie did. Don't be afraid to voice your convictions. Paul, it turned out, did like Katie and was rather intrigued with her. He called her for another date and a chance to begin anew. She agreed as long as he realized where she stood. They went on to have some good times together.

Sometimes friends or family members will try to "fix you up" with someone you do not know. With your consent, they arrange a date for you. This is what is known as a "blind date." You have never met the person, you probably have no idea what he or she looks like (except for descriptions), and you have no inkling as to what he or she is interested in. Blind dates can turn out to be a lot of fun, or they can be a real drag. If you agree to go on a blind date, keep an open mind. Don't expect your date to look like Tom Cruise or Whitney Houston, and don't be visibly disappointed when the person bears no resemblance to celebrities. The main thing to remember is you agreed to this date. So, try to enjoy getting out of the house and taking in a movie or having a bite to eat. If the two of you hit it off—terrific! If not, neither one of you has lost anything.

Going on a blind date is usually more fun when you double date; that is, when you go out with another couple. However, if you are out alone on a blind date, be yourself and don't try to make a huge impression. A fun date is one who is a good listener and good company. You might feel awkward at first, but your date probably will also. If you're worried about what to talk about on a blind date, there are a lot of "surface" subjects you can start out with: the schools you attend, your families, hobbies, sports, and the mutual friend who brought you together. Try to go with the flow, and it just may turn out to be an enjoyable evening.

In the following situation, see how Linda reacts to the idea of a blind date and then see what actually happens on the date itself.

The door to the counselors' retreat cabin flew open and Danielle bounded into the room. A group of girls were sitting around chatting and sipping soft drinks.

"Guess what?" she said. "I just spoke to the director of Camp Duncan and she said the camp is going to have an appreciation party for the counselors. It's going to be in two weeks. And the best part of it all is . . ." She paused dramatically.

"What, Danielle?" demanded one of the girls. "Tell us!"

"Well," Danielle replied slowly with a sly smile sneaking around the corners of her mouth, "we can invite any boy we want. We can ask dates to come!"

"Ooh, that's fantastic!" cried Ellen. "I'm going

to write Mark tonight and ask him. What's the date and time?"

"It's going to be August 10th at 8:00," answered Danielle.

The girls talked excitedly among themselves about whom they would invite as well as what outfits they would wear. There was a boys camp three miles from Camp Duncan. The two camps often did outdoor activities together, so most of the girls knew many of the male counselors.

"Let's send out invitations," suggested a girl named Mindy. "We better do it soon in case any of us gets turned down. That way we can always ask someone else."

"Ooh, I'm going to ask Rick, you know, the tall guy with blond hair and blue eyes," said Jean dreamily. "He's such a hunk!"

"Who are you going to invite, Linda?" asked Mindy.

"Oh, I don't know," replied Linda hesitantly.

"Come on now, Linda," said Danielle. "You have to ask someone. We're all going with a date."

"I don't know if I'll go. I don't really know any of the guys from Camp Leeland. I'd feel stupid asking someone I don't even know."

"I have an idea," piped up Ellen, who had been busy making mental notes about how much fun it was going to be to have her steady boyfriend up at camp. "Why don't we fix you up with someone? You know . . . a blind date!"

"I've never been on a blind date before," answered Linda. "What if he turns out to be a total geek? I'd die!"

"Well, it's better than sitting alone in your cabin, isn't it?" said Danielle. "I think it's a great idea. Besides, if you don't like him, there will be plenty of other people there to talk to. It's not like you'd be stuck with him in a room all by yourself. C'mon, give it a try."

The rest of the girls supported what Danielle said and prompted Linda to agree.

"Okay, okay," she relented. "But I'm holding you personally responsible, Ellen!"

"Hey, that gives me an idea. Mark's cousin from Denver is visiting him this month. Why don't I have Mark ask him to come?"

"I guess that'll be okay," said Linda. "What does he look like?"

"Oh, he's 4' 10", weighs 400 pounds, has three eyes and purple hair," joked Ellen. "I don't know what he looks like, but if he's related to Mark, he can't be all bad!"

Once that was settled, the rest of the girls talked and made plans as to whom they would invite.

The date of the party rapidly approached. Each boy invited accepted the invitation. The girls were rather excited, everyone, that is, except Linda. She was apprehensive about her blind date.

As she and Ellen were getting ready for the party, Ellen said, "Loosen up, Linda. Everything will work out fine."

"Easy for you to say," replied Linda. "Oh my gosh, do you have any pimple cover-up? My forehead is all broken out."

"That's because you're so nervous," Ellen said, handing her the cream.

"Is this outfit okay?" asked Linda. "What should I do with my hair?"

"Relax. Your outfit is great. I wish I had your figure. Here. Use my combs in your hair." Ellen helped place the combs in Linda's hair.

The shrill blast of a car horn sounded outside the girl's cabin.

"They're here!" shrieked Ellen as she made a run for the door.

Linda took one last look in the mirror and thought, "Well, it's the best I can do." She took a deep breath and walked slowly toward the open door.

Mark and Ellen were engaged in a tight bear hug as Linda stepped out of the cabin. She cleared her throat loudly. The two broke apart.

"Oh, Linda, this is Mark. Mark, this is Linda."

"Hi, Linda. That's my cousin, Pete," said Mark, gesturing to the boy emerging from the car. "Pete, Linda."

The four exchanged greetings and walked into the cabin for a few minutes before going to the party. They made small talk for a while and Linda was grateful to have Ellen and Mark there. It made the blind date a little easier.

As they walked to the hall where the party was being held, Pete turned to Linda and said, "That's a neat outfit, Linda. You look nice."

Linda relaxed a bit and felt some of her anxiety slip away. "Thanks. You look nice too."

The party turned out to be quite a success. Linda and Pete got along pretty well and talked about their summer vacations, going back to school, and the different towns in which they lived. Ellen and Mark helped to put them both at ease.

That night while the girls changed into their pajamas, Ellen said to Linda, "Well, what did you think?"

"I'm glad he only had two eyes and brown hair," joked Linda.

"No, what did you really think?"

"Well, I'm not in love or anything. But he's a nice guy and I had a good time. He said he would call me after we get home from camp."

"When does he go back to Denver?"

"Not for another three weeks," yawned Linda with a happy sigh, as she turned out the light.

♥ eleven ♥

GOING STEADY

Going steady probably means something different at every school. Sometimes a boy and a girl consider themselves to be going steady (or "going together") if they talk a lot on the telephone. Perhaps they are steadies if they like each other a lot. Couples who are going steady sometimes walk each other to classes, hold hands in the halls, and go to parties together. It doesn't take long for the latest news of who is going steady with whom to hit the halls. And the same is true when any couple breaks up. People are likely to hear soon after it happens.

After a boy and girl have been dating for a period of time, they might consider themselves as going steady. Some people "go together" for a long time, others for a short time. Perhaps you don't want to be tied down to one steady girl or boy. You may wish to date different people. This is a decision for you to make.

How do you "break up" with someone? When young teenagers break up, it isn't as hard or as devastating as it might be for older adolescents. This is because the relationship doesn't generally last long, and no real dating has taken place. Because early adolescent relationships are so new, it's fun to get to know others. The number of phone calls from your steady may dwindle, the walking to classes together may become less frequent, and a mutual breakup occurs. You might want to talk to your steady and tell him or her you just don't want to go together any longer. You can always use your parents as an excuse; perhaps they think you are too young to go steady.

Breaking up doesn't mean you can't still be friends. However, it is harder to break up with someone when you are older. This is because you probably have been doing some actual dating, which makes the relationship more meaningful as well as closer. Ending a relationship like this might or might not be mutual. If only one of the two people involved wants to end it, the other is likely to be hurt. In a case such as this, it might be difficult to remain friendly with your ex-steady. It might be a tough situation to handle in the beginning, but as time goes on, you are bound to feel better. The key to dealing with a breakup is to acknowledge your feelings and then try to get busy. Get involved with activities that will help you meet other people.

Rejection—a feeling of being unwanted or excluded. It happens to everyone at one time or another. It could be a date rejection, a group rejection, a college rejection, or a job rejection. You may have summoned up all your courage to ask someone out, and when he or she said no, it felt like a kick in the pants. You felt like you wanted the ground to swallow you up, and yes, you felt like a jerk. This is all perfectly normal.

But how do you handle rejection? First, admit to yourself that you are feeling like this. Tell yourself it is okay to have this response toward rejection. Then try to think of something to do to get your mind off being upset. Go bowling with your buddies. Go roller-skating with your girlfriends. Talk to your best friend about your problem. Chances are you might get to laughing about it, and after a while you will forget how much it hurt. After being rejected, it might help to treat yourself to something. Buying a new sweater or new basketball might lift your spirits. A new hairstyle

might do the trick too. Do something for your ego, something that will make you feel good again.

Being rejected does not mean you are an unworthy person. There is an old expression that says "there is someone for everyone." Eventually, you will find him or her. In the meantime, there are a lot of "someones" who are not right for everyone. Being outgoing and caring about others, as well as being a good listener, will help you make more friends. Some people come by this naturally, while others have to work on feeling comfortable around their peers. Get back your self-confidence, do something nice for yourself, and that feeling of rejection will become a thing of the past.

Here is a situation about a boy named John who encounters rejection when he asks out a very popular girl named Lindsay.

The big eighth-grade fall dance was coming up in two weeks. John and his friend Kevin had talked about inviting dates to the dance. John was a little apprehensive because he had never asked anyone out before.

"Who would you like to take?" asked Kevin. "Lindsay Tate is a real fox. Why don't you call her?"

"I don't think she likes me," answered John. "Besides, I really don't know her."

"She's the best-looking girl on the tennis team," remarked Kevin. "She's not going with that sophomore anymore. Maybe she'd say yes."

"I don't know," hesitated John. "I'd feel like a geek if she said no. Why don't we just go by ourselves instead of with girls?"

"Oh, come on," prompted Kevin. "I'll ask Linda Morrow if you ask Lindsay Tate. We could go together. Linda and Lindsay are good friends."

"Okay. Okay. If you quit bugging me I'll call her. What should I say?"

"Just ask her if she wants to go to the dance with you. If she doesn't know who you are, tell her you're Tony Danza's brother," Kevin joked. "I'll look up her number for you."

John rolled his eyes and tried to think of what he would say to Lindsay. She was one of the most popular girls in his class, and John wasn't really "in" with her group. If she says no, John thought, I just won't go to the dance. He reached for the phone.

"Okay, Kevin, dial the number." John drew in a large breath. He signaled one ring with his finger. Two rings. Someone on the other end picked up the phone.

"Uh . . . hello. Is Lindsay there?" John managed to say.

"Just a minute, please," answered the other person.

Too quickly Lindsay's voice was heard. John's throat felt totally dry.

"Uh, Lindsay? This is John Taylor. Do you want to go to the fall dance with me?" John's face was beet red and his hands were all sweaty.

"John? Oh yeah, hi," replied Lindsay as she realized who it was. "Listen, I can't go with you. A group of my friends are all going together."

"Oh . . . okay, bye," stammered John, feeling like a big jerk.

Sensing his embarrassment, Lindsay quickly added, "Maybe I'll see you there."

"Well?" demanded Kevin after John hung up the phone. "What'd she say?"

John repeated the conversation to his friend.

"All right, so you got the big rejection. But she

didn't totally write you off. She did say maybe she'd see you there."

"Yeah, whoopee," said John flatly.

"Okay, maybe you were right. We'll just go with the guys," said Kevin. "That way we can fool around and see who's there. Just think, if Lindsay had said yes and you ended up taking her, maybe she'd be a big bore and you'd be stuck with her the whole night."

As it turned out, John and Kevin did go to the dance with a group of their friends. They had a good time, and John was asked to dance by a few girls. They weren't quite as popular as Lindsay, but they were nice and paid a lot of attention to John. John and his friends felt comfortable with these girls because they all seemed to be on the same social level.

Sometimes it's a good idea to ask out people who are within your own social boundaries, especially when you are new at dating. This will give you more confidence in your socializing ability. You might have more things in common and feel more at ease with people in your own group. Everyone feels awkward in new situations; boys as well as girls. If you start out by inviting the most popular girl or boy in your class for a date, you probably will feel even more awkward in terms of how you should act and what you should say. Once you have some dating experience under your belt, then you may be more comfortable asking out a really popular person. Ask yourself a question first: Do you want to go out with this person because he or she is fun to be with, or do you just want to improve your social situation? Will you have a good time with this person or are you only interested in looking good to your friends?

Being rejected by Lindsay did hurt John. But, he did himself a favor by going to the dance with his friends. The good time he had lifted his spirits and made him feel good about himself again.

Another type of rejection kids can encounter is rejection from within their peer group. It hurts when you are excluded. This type of rejection is not limited to adolescents. Children can experience it and so can adults. However, adolescents seem to feel the sting of peer group rejection more because it is very important for them to be accepted by others. See how Abby deals with this type of rejection in the following example.

Abby stood in the doorway as the huge empty moving van slowly made its way down the street. Her street. It didn't feel like her street. Nothing felt like hers anymore. Abby and her family had just moved from Seattle to New York. She left behind her friends, her school, and, yes, her street. She was in a different world now—all new and unfamiliar. She dreaded tomorrow when she had to go to school. Four weeks of seventh grade were left until summer vacation. Abby had wanted to start her new school in the fall, but her mother had insisted she go for the remaining four weeks. "Besides," her mom had said, "you'll make new friends at school."

The remainder of the school year passed rather slowly for Abby. She sort of liked a group of four girls and she tried making friends with them. She even had one of them over to her home after school a couple of times.

One afternoon after the dismissal bell rang, Abby kneeled, collecting books from her locker. As she was about to stand and close the door, she overheard two of her new "friends" talking.

"The sleepover is at Janet's house Friday night. Her mom is going to rent a video for us."

The other girl asked, "Who's going?" After hearing the names of the chosen few, the same girl added, "What about Abby? Wasn't she invited?"

"No, she's not really part of our group," came the biting answer.

Tears welling up in her eyes, Abby slammed her locker door and raced for the bus. Once home, she sobbed uncontrollably.

"Abby! Abby, what's wrong?" exclaimed her mother. After calming down, Abby repeated what she had overheard.

"It's awfully hard being new in school, isn't it?" comforted Mrs. Benson. "I'll tell you what. Let's look into the community swim team program for the summer. You are bound to meet some girls there who share your interests. Who knows? You might find someone through the team who likes the same sort of things you do."

Abby took her mother's advice and joined the swim team. She soon became friends with a girl who had similar interests.

Rejection from a peer group is tough to swallow. Talking to your parents or siblings might help you. Share your feelings. Perhaps someone can give you some good advice. Keep in mind that there are a lot of kids out there just waiting for a new friend to come along. It takes courage and a desire to get yourself involved with activities that will open the door to new friendships. Everyone usually finds his or her own niche and a group to whom he or she belongs. Discovering it might take some time. Perseverance pays.

CHAPTER

♥ thirteen ♥

DATING SURVEY INFORMATION

The next few pages include information gathered from questionnaires distributed to preteens and teens from California, Michigan, New York, and New Jersey. The ages of the boys and girls who responded to this questionnaire ranged from ten to fourteen years old. They were in the fifth, sixth, and seventh grades. Names were not included on the papers, which made for open and honest answers. You might want to answer the questions yourself (but don't write in the book!) and then read to see how other kids responded.

1. Age_____
2. Girl_____ Boy_____
3. If you are a girl, are you interested in making friends with boys?
   not interested_____ somewhat interested_____ very interested_____
4. If you are a boy, are you interested in making friends with girls?

not interested_____ somewhat
interested_____ very interested_____

5. Have you ever gone to a party where both girls and boys have been invited?
no_____ once_____ more than once_____

6. Would you *like* to go to parties where both girls and boys are invited?
no_____ maybe_____ yes_____

7. Have you ever gone to a dance or a "sock hop"?
no_____ yes_____

8. Have you ever asked someone of the opposite sex to go out with you?
no_____ yes_____

9. Have you ever been asked out by some-one of the opposite sex?
no_____ yes_____

10. Have you ever gone places (roller skat-ing, movies, bowling, etc.) with a group of boys and girls?
no_____ yes_____ If so, where?_____

11. At what age do you think dating is okay to start?_____
At what age do your parents think dat-ing is okay to start?_____

12. If you are a girl and you like a boy, how do you get him to notice you?_____
_____
_____

13. If you are a boy and you like a girl, how do you get her to notice you?_____
_____
_____

14. Have you or any of your friends ever "gone steady"?_____

15. What does "going steady" mean to you?

_____
_____
_____

16. Where would you like to go if you went out on a date?_____

_____

How would you get there?_____

_____

17. Would you feel more comfortable going places with a group of your friends (boys and girls) rather than going on a single date? Explain._____

_____
_____

18. If you asked someone out and he or she said no, how would you feel?_____

_____

19. Girls- Please list the qualities you like in boys. (ex: friendly, sense of humor, looks, etc.)_____

_____

20. Boys- Please list the qualities you like in girls. (ex: friendly, sense of humor, looks, etc.)_____

_____

21. Would you like information on these topics in this book?
    _____how to get a boy/girl to notice me
    _____how to act around boys/girls
    _____how to get a group of boys and girls together
    _____where to go with a group of boys and girls
    _____how to ask someone out
    _____where to go on a single date

_____permission from parents to do
things with a group of kids
_____permission from parents to sin-
gle date
_____dating an older person
_____dating and peer pressure
_____personal hygiene (cleanliness,
grooming)

What other things would you like discussed in a
dating book for preteens? Your thoughts will be
very helpful to me. Please use this space to write
down comments and questions.

The majority of girls said they were very interested in making friends with boys. Boys were
evenly split between somewhat and very interested in making friends with girls. A few responded they were not interested at all. These answers seem to support the notion that girls are
usually more mature and ready for opposite sex
friendships than boys at this age. The younger
boys questioned (ages 10 and 11) were the ones
who were not interested at all.

Most of the kids surveyed had gone to parties
where both girls and boys had been invited. Again,
it was the older girl and boy who said yes to the
question, while a few younger preteens had not
gone to coed parties. More than 75 percent of the
kids said they would like to go to boy/girl parties.

Less than half of the girls (38 percent) had attended a dance or sock hop. Only 28 percent of
the boys had attended a dance or sock hop. Because most kids surveyed were still in grade school,
this leads one to suspect that dances are more
common in junior high school or middle school.

For questions eight and nine, it was again the

HE PULLED UP HIS EYELIDS
UNTIL THEY WERE INSIDE OUT,
HAD PENCILS HANGING
OUT OF HIS EARS, AND
MADE A HORRIBLE SOUND
WITH HIS NOSE —
I'M IN LOVE !!

ANNE CANEVARI GREEN 89

older kids who said they had either asked out or had been asked out by someone of the opposite sex.

The age at which preteens and teens thought dating was okay varied between ten and fifteen years of age. The kids thought their parents would allow dating anywhere between twelve and sixteen years old. Some kids did not know how their parents felt about this.

In order to get a boy to notice her, the girls wrote they "flirt, act friendly and be nice, write notes, call him, ask help with homework, hang around him, or ask friends to ask him if he likes her." The boys wrote "be funny, act nice, show off, look at her, call her, dress nicely, or ask her for a homework assignment even if they already knew it."

The majority of the girls or their friends and the boys or their friends have gone steady.

The girls had different answers about what going steady meant. The various answers were: "going with one person," "talking on the phone," "going to parties together," "seeing each other after school," "wearing a class ring or the boy's jacket," "holding hands," "studying together," and "sometimes kissing." The boys responses were: "holding hands," "going with one person," "not flirting with anyone else." Some boys didn't know what going steady meant.

The question of where you would like to go if you went on a date was answered by: the movies, pizza parlor, roller-skating, or parties. Most boys and girls said parents or older siblings would drive them. Some said they would walk or meet there. One boy wrote he would like to go to Florida on a date and would get there by jet!

The majority of boys and girls would prefer to go on a "group date." The reasons for this varied from feeling more comfortable, wouldn't be embarrassed or nervous, to there would be more people to talk to, and they would feel safer. A few kids thought going on a single date would be preferable because they'd get to know their date better and they would feel no pressure from the group.

When questioned how they would feel if they asked someone out and he or she said no, the boys and girls responded: embarrassed, sad, hurt, fine, disappointed, rotten, let down, and stupid. Some girls and boys said they would ask someone else out. As one boy put it, "There are a lot more girls around."

The qualities in boys that girls find appealing were: looks, friendliness, sense of humor, smart, caring, and not being a show-off. The qualities in girls that boys liked were: friendliness, looks, sense of humor, being smart, kind, not being a snob, and being understanding.

Remember . . . there are no right and wrong answers to this questionnaire. Although many answers were similar, no two people responded exactly the same way. Every individual has his or her own opinions.

Some preteens and teens had questions about dating. Included are those that might be of particular interest to you, the reader.

• "What do you do if you like a guy, but your best friend is already going with him?" First of all, you have to remember how important your friendship is with your girlfriend. You probably have a "crush" on her boyfriend and crushes usually don't last very long. Do you like him enough to risk your friendship with your best friend? At this age, preteen boyfriend/girlfriend relationships don't last that long, so why not wait and see what happens with them in the next few weeks? They might break up, and then you would be free to pursue a friendship with him. Sometimes guys you "can't have" seem more appealing than other guys. Wait and see what happens before you jeopardize your friendship with your best friend.

• "How do you break up with someone without hurting him? And how can you still be friends with him?" Talk the situation over with your boyfriend. See if you both can reach an understanding. Sometimes this is hard to do, but whatever you decide, remember "time heals all wounds." Act friendly toward him, but don't overdo it or he'll think you want to get back together.

• "How do I handle my friends when they don't like my boyfriend? They tease me." Maybe your friends are jealous of you. It's hard for you because you want to spend time with your boyfriend as well as with your girlfriends. And they in turn probably want to do things with you, but perhaps you seem too busy. Make an effort to set time aside for your girlfriends. Try not to let your boyfriend take up all your time. Talk to your friends about the teasing. Maybe they are unaware they are hurting you.

• "I'm the baby of the family. How do I get my parents to not treat me as such?" Show them how responsible you are. Perhaps you could start baby-sitting for neighbors. When they see you are caring for other babies and children, maybe they'll realize *you* are no longer a baby.

• "How long does it take a boy to notice me?" Hopefully, if you like him, it won't take long. Get

yourself involved with things he might be involved in. Find an area that you think you excel in and work on it. When you are good at something, people usually take notice. Don't forget—being friendly and saying "hi" to him won't hurt.

• "When is it okay for a boy and a girl to kiss?" If kissing makes you feel uncomfortable, then it is not okay, whether you are 12, 35, or 102! Don't let friends pressure you into kissing or making out with your girlfriend or boyfriend. Kissing is a personal decision, one that only you can make.

• "How do I let this girl know I like her?" Try a little friendliness. Say hello, smile at her, and try starting a conversation about something you think she'd be interested in.

• "How should I act on a date? What should I say?" First dates always make *both* people involved nervous. Be yourself—that's why the person is going out with you. He or she likes you just the way you are. What to talk about? School events, activities either of you is interested in, your family, schoolwork, extracurricular activities. Once you get going, the conversation will come more easily.

Thinking about dating, talking about dating, and actually "group" dating or single dating opens up an exciting new chapter in your life. All of the issues that have been discussed in this book are important ingredients in helping you discover who you are and what type of people you like and want to be with. Getting to know and becoming friends with members of the opposite sex—whether it is a platonic (nonromantic) friendship or a romantic friendship—helps pave the way to young adulthood and the formation of healthy, happy, lasting relationships.

Ultimately, you are the one to take charge of yourself and make certain decisions. As one twelve-year-old preteen wrote in the survey, "I think that teenage dating is all right as long as the teens don't fool around. Because I think that some teens don't realize that AIDS is a dangerous disease. Girls also can get pregnant at a young age, and I think it's stupid for a kid to have a kid."

So make the right choices, and above all, be yourself. Enjoy this special time in your life called adolescence and the peaks and valleys that go along with it. Make the transition from childhood to young adulthood a positive and rewarding experience.

FOR FURTHER READING

Booher, Diane D. *Love*. New York: Julian Messner, 1985.

Cahn, Julie. *The Dating Book*. New York: Julian Messner, 1983.

Comfort, Alex, and Jane Comfort. *The Facts of Love: Living, Loving and Growing Up*. New York: Crown Publishers, Inc., 1979.

Johnson, Corrine, and Eric Johnson. *Love and Sex and Growing Up*. New York: Bantam Books, 1979.

Johnson, Eric W. *Love and Sex in Plain Language*. New York: Bantam Books, 1979.

Winship, Elizabeth C. *Ask Beth*. Boston: Houghton Mifflin Co., 1976.

For information on sexually transmitted diseases, including referrals to clinics, call this national toll-free number:

800-227-8922

(American Social Health Association)

INDEX